Poems

from the

Heart

NORMA NAZARETH

Table of Contents

Poems from the Heart

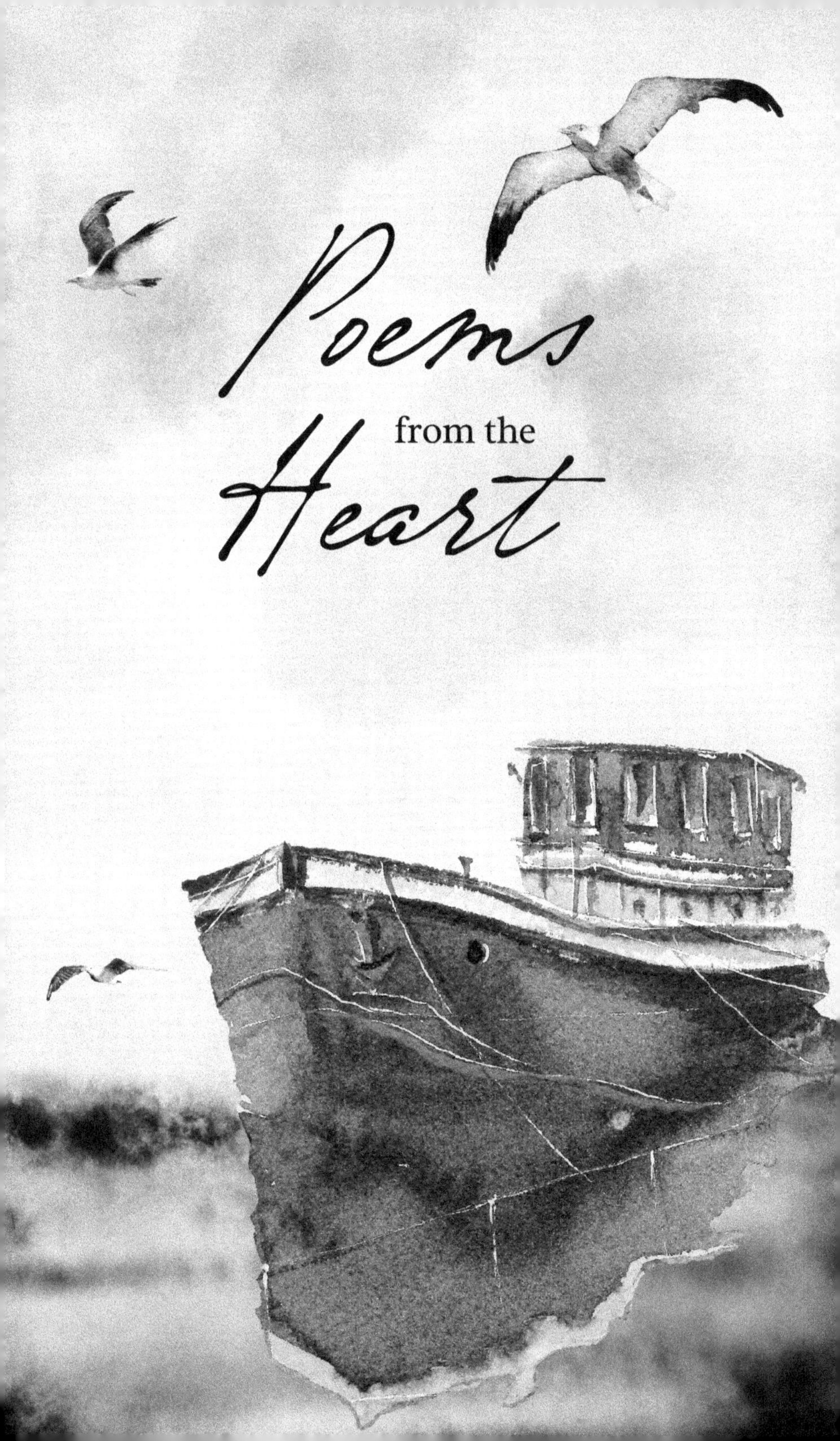

Dedication

At the very outset, let me give glory to God, the Father, His Son, Jesus, and the Holy Spirit. All of the writing in this book was made possible by the Holy Spirit working in my life to save, cleanse, sanctify, and make whole the work on the cross at Calvary, accomplished by Jesus, my Saviour and Lord. This book is a precious gift from the Lord to me, and through me to you.

Introduction

Poems from the Heart was birthed in the furnace of affliction, fired in God's furnace of discipling and disciplining, moulded in His hands of perfection, and shaped by His arms of love.

Each of God's words is like a diamond, multi-faceted and multi-dimensional. The same Word has an answer to each of our differing individual circumstances and ministers to the different dimensions of our being—spirit, mind, emotions, will (soul), and body. My most profound growth has been in the area of submitting my will and my mind to the Lord since I was an independent and rebellious person by nature, before coming to know the Lord Jesus personally as Saviour and Lord. God can change our hearts of stone and give us hearts of flesh if we so desire and allow Him.

I have come to realize that God had to send His Son Jesus to reveal to me, through Jesus' life, who He is by nature and how to obey His will, which Jesus did so perfectly. His death on the cross at Calvary for all of mankind accomplished His Father's will and gave me a second chance to choose between eternal life or death, Heaven or hell.

Man, by nature, born in sin and shapen in iniquity, has a propensity to quickly turn things into idols and gods, whether they be images, idols, self (new age), or lifestyles. We are quick to worship the created, the work of our hands and hearts, instead of the Creator. Jesus and His Word are God's standard of Godly living. I have had to release all of my ideas, attitudes, and notions that contradict the Holy Bible.

The Bible says, "taste and see that the Lord is good" (Psalm 34:8a). The more I soak in His Word and meditate upon it, the more it changes me since it is "living and powerful, and sharper than any two-edged sword" (Hebrews 4:12a). The Word (Jesus) is life, and life is in His blood, which was shed for me at Calvary. By faith in Jesus alone, I have appropriated that eternal life. So, I have the assurance of divine transfusion of Jesus' life in my life by the Holy Spirit, as I choose to obey and live by God's will and not mine. It is not easy, but possible by God's mercy and grace. I am by no means perfect, and this process of sanctification will go on till I meet my Master, but I am on my journey of learning to worship God in Spirit and Truth.

I hope with all my heart that this book blesses you richly as it has blessed me. God gave me my first poem (I call it my testimony poem) in February 1999, when He started healing me spiritually and bringing me into wholeness in Him. I had a wounded and crushed spirit that needed only the Maker's divine touch.

If you do not know Jesus as Saviour and Lord, I pray the Holy Spirit will anoint each word and draw your heart to your loving Heavenly Father who made you, shaped you, loves you, and desires fellowship with you eternally in Heaven. The most touching element of the Gospel is "love" in that, "while we were still sinners, Jesus died for us" (Romans 5:8), and "God so loved the world that He gave His only begotten Son that whosoever believes in Him should not perish but have eternal life" (John 3:16). Won't you choose Jesus today? Life and not death? Heaven and not hell?

To do this, you simply need to acknowledge you are a sinner in need of a Saviour. Repent and ask God to forgive you and cleanse you of your sin. Accept by faith the sinless blood of Jesus shed on the cross at Calvary as the price paid for your redemption and ask Jesus to come into your life. Acknowledge Him as Your Saviour and Lord. Read the Holy Bible daily and find a Spirit-filled church. There, you will learn to grow from a babe in Christ into a mature Christian living for Jesus.

Surrender all to Him and live for Him from this day forth. Today is the day of your salvation! You will live in peace and joy despite your trials and tribulations and enjoy blessings like you have never experienced before.

May the love of God overwhelm you as you enjoy His presence. God's abundant blessings always!

Norma

Guiding Scriptures of My Christian Walk

And they overcame him by the blood of the Lamb
and by the word of their testimony,
and they did not love their lives to the death.
—Revelation 12:11

And now abide faith, hope, love, these three;
but the greatest of these is love.
—1 Corinthians 13:13

But seek first the kingdom of God and His righteousness,
and all these things shall be added to you.
—Matthew 6:33

Blessed are those who hunger and thirst for righteousness,
For they shall be filled.
—Matthew 5:6

Blessed are the pure in heart, For they shall see God.
—Matthew 5:8

Who may ascend into the hill of the Lord? Or who may stand in
His holy place? He who has clean hands and a pure heart, Who
has not lifted up his soul to an idol, Nor sworn deceitfully.
—Psalm 24:3–4

Has the Lord as great delight in burnt offerings and sacrifices,
As in obeying the voice of the Lord? Behold, to obey is better
than sacrifice, And to heed than the fat of rams. For rebellion is
as the sin of witchcraft, And stubbornness is as iniquity and
idolatry. Because you have rejected the word of the Lord, He
also has rejected you from being king.
—1 Samuel 15:22–23

For in Him we live and move and have our being, as also some of
your own poets have said, "For we are also His offspring."
—Acts 17:28

Then Jesus said to His disciples, "If anyone desires to come after Me,
let him deny himself, and take up his cross, and follow Me.
—Matthew 16:24

"Not everyone who says to Me, 'Lord, Lord,' shall enter the
kingdom of heaven, but he who does the will of My Father in
heaven. Many will say to Me in that day, 'Lord, Lord, have we not
prophesied in Your name, cast out demons in Your name, and done
many wonders in Your name?' And then I will declare to them, 'I
never knew you; depart from Me, you who practice lawlessness!'"
—Matthew 7:21–23

But the fruit of the Spirit is love, joy, peace, longsuffering, kindness,
goodness, faithfulness, gentleness, self-control.
Against such there is no law.
—Galatians 5:22–23

Let your conduct be without covetousness; be content
with such things as you have. For He Himself has said,
"I will never leave you nor forsake you."
—Hebrews 13:5

Most assuredly, I say to you, unless a grain of wheat
falls into the ground and dies, it remains alone; but
if it dies, it produces much grain.
—John 12:24

Poems of Salvation

Jesus, My Saviour and Lord

Pour out on me, Lord, Your mercy and grace,
as I go through each day beholding Your face.
With eyes so tender, heart so compassionate and true,
Giving strength to my walk as I abide in You.

For You truly are the vine, and I am the branch
that will wither and die if I leave You by chance.
I know where I was, and thank You, truly I do,
for revealing Yourself to me till I cried, "I need You."

You showed me I could not make it through life alone,
except by leaning on You and coming to Heaven's throne.
There You sit, as High Priest, as My Saviour and Lord,
presenting my petitions before dear Father God.

Thank You, dear Jesus, for being patient with me
till I bowed my knee and humbled myself before Thee.
I now have the confidence, and assurance too,
that no one can snatch me out of Your hand while I rest in You.

My life was a mess till I met You,
You transformed and gave me a peace,
and now nothing else will do.
Despite my troubles and storms, You are there by my side,
My Saviour and Friend, withholding the tide.

Eternal life, blessings, health, and joy are for me,
when You shed Your blood on Calvary's tree.
Salvation is mine and my family's too,
That's what Your Word promises, and I trust in You.

You are my Husband and Guide and Counsellor too.
You sent your Holy Spirit to teach me to stay true.
I thank You for being in my boat each day,
on my way to Heaven, as I sail Earth's way.
The enemy is on the run as I walk in Your strength,
My Faithful Saviour, Lord, and Wonderful Friend.

And lo, I am with you always,
even to the end of the age.
—Matthew 28:20b

You Need the Saviour, the Lord Jesus

Man, by nature, is rebellious and proud.
The little he knows, he yells out loud.
He formulates his own philosophies and theories,
makes God fit into his mould of mental imageries.

Man loves his ego and enjoys his sin.
Pride and pleasure lead him to eternal ruin.
Man's life on earth is fleeting like a flower,
in bloom today and washed by tomorrow's shower.

Man prefers to believe the lies of the enemy.
He thinks his good works will earn him Heavenly entry.
God is going to ask on judgement day,
"Whom did you believe in? What do you have to say?"

The Bible declares the penalty for sin is death.
Jesus paid our price to give us eternal spiritual breath.
What pride in man's heart if he thinks his good deeds
will take him to Heaven, he alone in the lead.

No Saviour before him, he's his own caretaker.
He's in charge of his life, forsaking his Maker.
There is no hope for such arrogance,
eternal death awaits such ignorance.

My prayer for you, as you read this book,
is to get a glimpse of Jesus, whom on the cross Heaven forsook.
On Calvary, in unconditional love, He undertook
to put your name in His life's book.

So arise, man, awaken from your slumber
before it is too late to realize your blunder.
Jesus is the only Way, the Truth and the Life,
He revealed His Father and bought you a new life.

May the Holy Spirit soften your heart to hear
the love of the Saviour beckoning you to draw near.
May He open your eyes to see
He is the only doorway for free entry.

May His words fall on the rich soil of your heart,
bringing forth an abundant harvest right from the start.
May you thirst for His Presence ever so real,
sensing His peace, love, and joy that are priceless pearls.

Life apart from Him is shallow;
your spirit will run dry tomorrow.
Enjoyment is only fleeting;
it will leave your heart broken and bleeding.

Come now before it is too late.
The Saviour's open arms to you are the only gate.
His love is unconditional and passionate for you.
May your heart burn with desire for His love too.

I have come as a light into the world, that whoever believes in Me should
not abide in darkness. And if anyone hears My words and does not believe,
I do not judge him; for I did not come to judge the world but to save the
world.
—John 12:46–47

Jesus

J
is for Jesus, who from Heaven came.

E
is for earth, where to, He came.

S
is for sin, which to conquer, He came.

U
is for us, who trust in His name.

S
is for Saviour, who took away our sin and shame,
and that's why Jesus, our Saviour came.

Then the angel said to them, "Do not be afraid, for behold,
I bring you good tidings of great joy which will be to
all people. For there is born to you this day in the city
of David a Savior, who is Christ the Lord."

—Luke 2:10–11

Testimony of a Boat Christened "Norma"

On a day in September, the year I won't tell,
a boat christened "Norma" was headed for Port Hell.
I appointed myself captain; that seemed the best thing to do.
No one else would root for me; that's what I thought too.

I steered my boat, through calm and many stormy nights,
without a compass to guide and no real light.
Off course, I thought, I had it all right,
not realizing, to God, I was a pathetic sight.

The years went by; my boat went its merry way,
loading up ungodly cargo, leading me further astray.
Through the foolishness of pride, my boat puffed beyond the limit,
not realizing through God's eyes, I was not a giant but a mere midget.

A false sense of self-sufficiency crept into my heart.
It started to wear down the engine unnoticeably at the start.
Personal events began to happen, tossing my boat in its winds,
without light, navigator, and compass, do you think I could win?

I realized I needed God if I were to change course,
I docked at Port Repentance one Sunday in church, of course.
In an instant, the Word of God healed my blurry sight;
it dispelled the darkness of my soul as I saw the Saviour's light.

Suddenly, His overwhelming light made everything so crystal clear.
I had been steering in darkness through all these many years.
I looked at myself and saw the condition of my ship;
it required a skillful surgeon to reconstruct,
like Jacob, my wounded hip.

I saw the loving arms of the Saviour open wide to enfold me,
it was His blood on the cross of Calvary that bought me eternity.
Tears streamed down my face as I realized His love lifted me.
God suffered to send His only Son to include me in His family.

Gratitude and love flooded my broken, sinful heart.
Now "Born Again," I realized He loved me, right from the start.
My boat was creaking, junk laden, and needed lots of repair;
at Port Salvation, I almost gave up in hopelessness and despair.

My ungodly cargo, I knew I had to jettison,
if I were to lighten my load to ease my burden.
My course was changed that very day;
henceforth, I had the Holy Spirit to lead and guide the way.

He promised to change my boat and refashion me into a ship.
If I let Him, it was going to be a challenging but exciting trip.
From Port Salvation, we sailed that day in peace and joy,
through the long Port Sanctification,
where with other ships I travel in convoy.

I was to be a service boat that docked at the Holy Spirit's command,
picking up passengers on the way who needed a helping hand.
That day, the cleansing process would begin;
through surrender, obedience, and forgiveness,
He was going to lift my chin.

The early part of the voyage was painful, and boy, did it ever hurt!
Winds blew, and tempests rocked my boat; He was cleaning out the dirt.
With determination, I anchored my rudder to His precious, Holy Word.
I was not going to give in to the enemy—his lies were for the birds.

Occasionally, there were valleys and
meadows on either side of the stream.
It was so joyous and peaceful, cruising as if I were in a dream.
I eagerly listened and watched, soaking up His words,
Not wanting anything to be lost or stolen by the birds.

At other times, He led my boat through forests, dense and thick.
I could not discern His presence, crying out to Him in panic.
The legalistic spirit mocked me, that I had lost God's favour.
Praying was futile, a waste of time because Jesus is not my Saviour.

It was a tough fight through many a dark night,
sometimes at the edge of a cliff,
holding on to the Word for comfort and sight,
lest despair would sink my ship.
Then suddenly, His Word burst forth with light,
and ushered in a brand new day.
Then I saw He was always with me,
though I thought He had gone away.

In time, the Saviour began to reveal the immensity of His love,
precious and unique, always falling fresh from above.
I am as important to Him as the other boats alongside me,
He is cheering us onward on our course to our eternal destiny.

We are enlisted in God's navy; Jesus is Captain of our fleet.
Our course is a spiritual battle;
we have to persevere and not retreat.
The nature and destination of our boat is changed,
by God's grace and mercy,
mine was changed from a boat christened "Norma,"
to a ship sailing to Port Heaven, in glory.
From Port Repentance to Port Salvation
to Port Heaven via Port Sanctification,
this is God's plan for man's sin remedy
and man's eternal destiny.

Jesus answered, "Most assuredly, I say to you, unless one is born of water
and the Spirit, he cannot enter the kingdom of God."
—John 3:5

Home At Last

I remember that day when I bowed my heart to You,
when I cried and said, "Lord, I need You."
I looked up and saw none other than You,
with arms outstretched saying, "Come, I love you."
I have never regretted that day I lay nestled close to Your heart,
Completely assured I am home at last!

He brought me to the banqueting house,
And his banner over me was love.
—Song of Solomon 2:4

In Heaven's Light

In Heaven's light, a sinner I was,
in Heaven's light, condemned to hell I was.
In Heaven's light, there was no hope for me,
if I did not trust Jesus to set me free.
And now,
In Heaven's love, a saint I am,
in Heaven's love, on my way to glory, I am.
With a spirit anew and a heart that is blest,
Jesus paid the price, for my eternal rest.

For all have sinned and fall short of the glory of
God, being justified freely by His grace through the
redemption that is in Christ Jesus.
—Romans 3:23–24

My Child. Norma

"Norma, Norma, My child,
it is now time to hear.
I have been calling out to you,
through all these years.

Your eyes have been blinded,
your ears blocked too;
you haven't been able to hear My voice,
calling out to you.

As My child, you thought
I didn't care;
because people failed you,
you thought I wasn't there.

You sat in church,
sorrowed and cried;
you didn't know
I bottled every tear that dried.

Your life, you thought, was one of
sorrow, hopelessness, and despair,
that shriveled your spirit,
and left you bare.

Through all these years,
you looked for the water of life,
you drank at many wells,
but found only restlessness and strife.

You chose ungodly beliefs
to hide the pain
and ungodly behaviours
that gave the enemy free reign.

You built thick walls around you, my child,
that no one could dynamite,
but my Holy Spirit inside.

I gave you free will, you see, that no one can override.
No, not even Me.
You need to take off your sandals when you approach Me.
Shake the dust off your feet when you deal with Me.

I have longed to comfort you
these many years,
hug and caress you,
and wipe away your tears.

You always had
a special place in My heart,
tender and loving,
right from the start.

I gave you My Holy Spirit,
to lead you and guide,
to be co-heir with Jesus,
His beautiful bride.

You are accepted and chosen
and unconditionally too.
My Son paid the price—
it was also for you.

Come to Me,
open, honest, and real.
Talk to Me,
you are My precious pearl.

I have healed your pain
and made you whole.
You can stop striving,
for you have reached your goal.

I love you tenderly.
I am always near;
draw your strength from Me.
You need never fear.

Listen to My heartbeat,
respond to My love.
Sit at my feet—
I will teach you, My dove.

I am your "Abba" Father,
who has revealed His heart.
This was My intention,
right from the start.

I am marinating and seasoning you
in My heart, full of love and grace,
as you walk through the fires of life,
radiating the glory of My face.

Trust in the Lord with all your heart,
And lean not on your own understanding;
In all your ways acknowledge Him,
And He shall direct your paths.
—Proverbs 3:5–6

My Blessed Saviour

Into the misty distance, I peered and saw;
it was my Blessed Saviour, at whom I gazed in awe.

The chasm was deep, the gap was wide.
The price was high to go to the other side.

Then suddenly, I noticed His cross bridging the gap,
from earth to Heaven, from me to His lap.

I stumbled to the cross and fell down at His feet,
repented and begged for mercy, as I realized His feat.

The Saviour was sinless, my price was on His brow.
I acknowledged Him, Saviour and Lord, my knee I had to bow.

His love enveloped me, I started to cry.
It was for me, He went to Calvary to die.
I said, "Let me be Your lamb, I pray,
always in Your fold, never to stray."

"The choice is yours," He said to me,
"I am always faithful, and won't you be?"
"Teach me faithfulness," I said, "and how to be true
to turn to none other but only You."

And the Word became flesh and dwelt among us, and
we beheld His glory, the glory as of the only
begotten of the Father, full of grace and truth.
—John 1:14

From Death to Life

The mark of death and destruction, we see all around;
the consequences of sin, are everywhere to be found.
Whether in animals, fish, plants, or birds of the air,
you have only to look, and you will see death's stare.

There are the predators, and there are the hunted;
there are the criminals who terrorize the haunted.
This is the work of the enemy, who infiltrated from outer space,
through deceit took man's dominion over earth, given by God's grace.

When Adam and Eve in the Garden of Eden fell,
we came under the curse but have a choice for Heaven or hell.
Are we to choose God and accept His grace,
or choose the enemy and live forever in disgrace?

We were all struggling in darkness, thinking we were free.
It was some kind soul who prayed for our spiritual eyes to see.
The Father, in His mercy, from Heaven, sent His only Son
to die on Calvary and pay the ransom for everyone.

When we hear God's Word, we can choose to repent or rebel—
rebelliousness is a mark of the ungodly, destined to hell.
Repentance is a mark of the righteous, quick to answer God's call,
willing to lose their lives and surrender their all.

They obey God's will, allowing Him to lead and guide,
they stop striving and allow Him to control the tide.
Troubles may come and persecutions too.
They know their God will not forsake them but see them through.

Man's life is a living hell; you see it in the young and the old.
Till man surrenders his life to Jesus,
there is a miserable story to be told.
When he is born again, then you should behold his face,
from tears to joy, reflecting the glory of the Father's grace.

All creation is groaning,
waiting for the Saviour to return
to restore all Godly order and perfection.
No more enemies, our souls to churn.
No tears, no sorrow, no sickness, no pain,
Father, Son, and Holy Ghost, our eternal gain.

And God will wipe away every tear from their eyes;
there shall be no more death, nor sorrow, nor crying.
There shall be no more pain, for the former
things have passed away.
—Revelation 21:4

Jesus, the Only Difference

Jesus is the only difference
'cause He alone lights the way.
He shows up the darkness
as He brightens each day.

Other religions think
man's good works bring salvation.
Jesus did the redemptive work on the cross.
Will we accept His invitation?

To compare our good works with that of the sinless Lamb
is foolishness and a lie.
Why can't we trust Him
to move us from death to eternal life?

The world without Him
is in chaos and despair.
With the life of Jesus,
who can compare?

His Spirit and Word transforms and energizes
to enthrone Him and lay all else aside.
His Spirit and Word convicts and cleanses
to present us spotless as His bride.

As Moses would not take a step
without the presence of the Master,
how can we expect to be good?
A life of selfishness only brings disaster.

Let us surrender and love Him with all of our being,
'cause God created us to obey our King.
We will be fruitful and bring Him glory.
Without Him, only death, in a stand-alone theory.

Collectively, let us burn bright, with the fire of His love,
that He so mercifully pours out on us each day from above.
When the lost see us, they will immediately know
Jesus is the Only Difference and you bet it shows.

But those who wait on the Lord
Shall renew their strength;
They shall mount up with wings like eagles,
They shall run and not be weary,
They shall walk and not faint.
—Isaiah 40:31

Poems of Sanctification

Lump of Clay

Look what You did with this hapless lump of clay.
You are shaping and filling me to worship and pray.
When I first trusted You, You allowed me to fall
and break into a thousand pieces: lock, stock, barrel, and all.
You showed me the chinks in my armor so weak,
as I fell from my pedestal and started to squeak.
I thank You, Dear Lord, for the work You have begun,
for You will see me through till the day I am done.
I can't wait for Heaven to serve my Master and Lord,
face to face in the presence of an Eternal God.
Walking the streets of gold in a body anew,
no tears, no sorrow, no heartache,
Just You.

Therefore, if anyone is in Christ, he is a new creation;
old things have passed away; behold, all things have become new.
—2 Corinthians 5:17

Fruit of Heaven

In the garden of my heart, among the plants and the trees
blows the wind of the Holy Spirit all day,
sometimes strong, sometimes mild, sometimes cool, sometimes hot,
as I open my heart to Heaven.

Jesus shows me and convicts me
of the trees I should prune, of the ones I should cut down and burn,
so that the only ones that grow, mature, and flourish
are the ones that can bear fruit for Heaven.

There are times I cry and say, "Dear Lord,
that tree I do not want to have pruned."
Though it weighs my heart with sorrow and pain
and bears no good fruit for Heaven."

But to Him, at last, must I give in and say,
"You know what is best for me,
for only You have unconditional love for me
and an agenda that is only of Heaven."

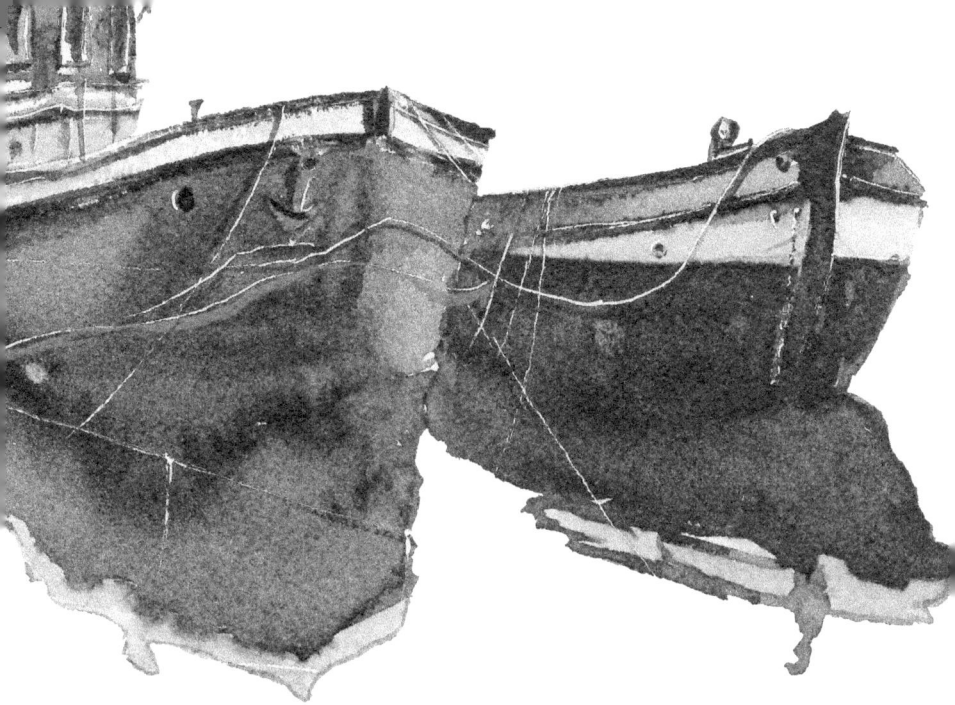

It is so pleasant to meet with my Saviour and Lord
as He entwines His arms into mine
and talks and whispers of His love divine
and the love of His Father in Heaven.

Thank you, Dear Jesus, for taking the time
to spend in the garden of my heart
for You truly are the Lily and the Rose of Sharon
that can fill me with the love of Heaven.

But the fruit of the Spirit is love, joy, peace,
longsuffering, kindness, goodness, faithfulness,
gentleness, self-control. Against such there is no law.
—Galatians 5:22–23

My Life on Earth

My life on earth has been one of sorrow, tears and shame;
despair and distress have been the name of the game.
You truly have set me free to lean on no one but You,
emptying my earthly treasure and filling it with You.

Take My yoke upon you and learn from Me, for I am gentle and lowly in
heart, and you will find rest for your souls.
For My yoke is easy and My burden is light.
—Matthew 11:29–30

But a Shell

Lord, You know who I am, nothing but a shell,
from whom You are purging all morass and hell.
You are filling me now and making me new,
attaching me to You with Holy Spirit glue.

"Clean Hands" and "Pure Heart"—well, that's what You need
to get my feet upon Your Holy hill and be freed.
Let my life be a blessing to others, as Yours has been to me,
as I lead others to Jesus, witnessing for Thee.

Who may ascend into the hill of the Lord?
Or who may stand in His holy place?
He who has clean hands and a pure heart,
Who has not lifted up his soul to an idol,
Nor sworn deceitfully.
—Psalm 24:3-4

In Heaven's Eyes

In Heaven's eyes we are such a sorry sight,
until we see the light,
By faith in One and One alone,
His name is Jesus Christ.
He left His majesty and throne
and came for you and me,
to move us out of darkness into light,
our home for all eternity.

Teach me, Lord, Your love divine,
a love selfless and true,
a love that shed its blood on the cross,
a love that purchased me too.
Help me love my fellow men,
whether they be black, white, or blue;
help me love unconditionally
and give as You give too.

Love suffers long and is kind; love does not envy; love does not
parade itself, is not puffed up; does not behave rudely, does not
seek its own, is not provoked, thinks no evil; does not rejoice in iniquity, but
rejoices in the truth; bears all things, believes all things, hopes all things,
endures all things. Love never fails.
—1 Corinthians 13:4–8a

My Path of Life

Once, I skipped down the path of life,
cobbled with stones of loneliness, fear, and strife.
I tripped and fell and upset the unity
of spirit, soul, and body, my God-given trinity.

Through all the loneliness, fear, darkness, and despair,
I cried out to the Lord, who answered my prayer.
He opened my eyes so that I could see,
His love and mercy that has since enveloped me.

Now, with joy, I skip down the path of life,
hand in hand with Jesus, free of strife.
He paid the price and unshackled me,
Released me from bondage and set me free.

Jesus said to him, "I am the way, the truth, and the life.
No one comes to the Father except through Me.
—John 14:6

What Are These Homes?

What are these homes that look so bright,
that glisten in the dark with a soft glow?
They are our hearts, the home of our Lord Jesus,
purchased at a price, now washed white as snow.

No rot can eat, no moth can enter,
For its doors are guarded and kept
Safe from thief, destroyer, and plunderer.
In peace, we have many a night slept.

Homes that are mobile and travel at ease,
not paid for in human price.
God's Son alone redeemed us for Him.
How precious the Lord's sacrifice!

Our homes are filled with the riches of Christ,
where robes of His righteousness shine.
They cover these filthy rags of ours,
not forgetting they are eternally divine.

So, come sweet Presence, and fill our hearts,
As we worship You with all-consuming passion.
Your glorious Son-shine will be seen by all men
Serving You, our earnest decision.

Coming to Him as to a living stone, rejected indeed by men, but
chosen by God and precious, you also, as living stones, are being
built up a spiritual house, a holy priesthood, to offer up
spiritual sacrifices acceptable to God through Jesus Christ.
Therefore it is also contained in the Scripture, "Behold, I lay
in Zion A chief cornerstone, elect, precious, And he who believes
on Him will by no means be put to shame." Therefore, to you
who believe, He is precious; but to those who are disobedient, "The
stone which the builders rejected Has become the chief cornerstone."
—1 Peter 2:4–7

The Master Potter

One day, as I gazed through the Potter's door,
I saw all kinds of pots strewn on the floor
Of various shapes, colours, sizes, and hues,
some broken, misshapen, and tarnished too.

He moved effortlessly and gracefully amongst the pots,
caressing, polishing, and finishing them off.
In the far corner, I saw a smoldering oven
in which they were baked and glazed by the dozen.

When they came out, I saw with shock
what the furnace did to the entire stock.
They were toughened and made fit.
They glistened and shone as if lit.

His eyes caught mine in an intense glance.
I knew instantly my meeting was not by chance.
He was waiting patiently for me
so that He could give me a new destiny.

He asked me if I wanted to be tried
in His furnace of love, to be purified.
"Oh!" I said, "Your fire scorches and burns.
I guess I will have to stay a mediocre urn."
"The choice is yours," He said to me.
"I control the heat and its intensity, trust Me."

"Oh! Lord, You are the Potter, and I am the clay.
Break me, mould me,
and remake me as I surrender to You, today.
There is no better place I'd rather be,
than in the hands of the Master Potter,
lovingly refashioning me."

The word which came to Jeremiah from the Lord, saying: "Arise
and go down to the potter's house, and there I will cause you
to hear My words." Then I went down to the potter's house, and
there he was, making something at the wheel. And the vessel
that he made of clay was marred in the hand of the potter; so
he made it again into another vessel, as it seemed
good to the potter to make.
—Jeremiah 18:1-4

Poems of Exhortation

Little Ducks

I sat by a pond in New Hampshire to pray,
swimming toward me were some ducks that day.
Lord, Your little messengers were so pretty to see,
as they came in convoy, to welcome me.

They were grey, with brown breasts, and green and blue hoods,
not a care in the world, as they foraged for food.
In stately elegance, they swam as they met with others that day,
one large family swimming in peaceful array.

Look at the birds of the air, for they neither sow nor
reap nor gather into barns; yet your heavenly Father
feeds them. Are you not of more value than they?
—Matthew 6:26

The Rose

What a pretty flower the rose is—
it blooms and smiles with a tenderness.
Did you notice the thorns on its stems?
The dewdrops on its petals sparkling like gems?
Both have been given by God above,
sorrow and joy intermingle with love.

Then Jesus said to His disciples, "If anyone desires to come after
Me, let him deny himself, and take up his cross, and follow Me.
—Matthew 16:24

Breath of Clean, Fresh Air

Sometimes, you find yourself in a forest thick,
all alone, wondering and feeling sick,
looking for ways to come out of there,
as you find yourself mauled by beasts of despair.

You desperately pray, to suddenly find
a breath of clean, fresh air, sweeping your mind.
It is so real, you turn around to see,
from where cometh the air, wafting over thee.

It is the wind of the Holy Spirit sent to comfort you;
knowing your plight, He soothes and whispers too.
You spend long hours in fellowship with Him,
talking of your fears and dreams within.

At the end of the time, you can scarcely believe
He led you out of the forest to a meadow green.
So cool, so refreshing, He coaxes you to drink
deep gulps of clean, fresh air that make you think
how blessed you are to have Him comfort your soul.
It is only He who can pull you out of that desperate hole!

But the Helper, the Holy Spirit, whom the Father will send in
My name, He will teach you all things, and bring to your
remembrance all things that I said to you. Peace, I leave with
you, My peace I give to you; not as the world gives do I give to
you. Let not your heart be troubled, neither let it be afraid.

—John 14: 26-27

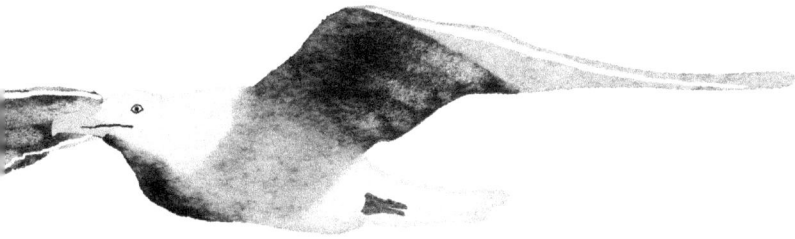

Reach for Jesus

Reach for Jesus, the bright Morning Star,
Reach for Jesus, always near and never far.
Reach for Jesus, a whisper of a prayer away,
Reach for Jesus, there even after trouble ebbs away.
Reach for Jesus, whom else would you want to know?
Reach for Jesus, who knew you before the word go.

For He Himself has said,
"I will never leave you nor forsake you."
—Hebrews 13:5b

Lessons from a Candle

The candle burned brightly
in a dark, cold room,
shedding its light warmly
I wonder, for whom?

Next morning, I saw it
lying wasted and spent,
lifeless and formless
wondering, where its short life went.

Then, the Lord whispered,
saying gently to me,
"Like this candle, My dear,
would you like to be?

Left to your own imaginings,
that's where you will end.
Without energy or individuality
lifeless and spent.

If I spark your fire,
it will well up from deep within,
with no other desire
than burn for your Glorious King.

Your flame, no man can snuff out.
On your flame, the enemy will surely blow.
But fear not, My child,
My Holy Spirit will always direct your glow."

In the beginning was the Word, and the Word was with God, and
the Word was God. He was in the beginning with God. All things
were made through Him, and without Him nothing was made that
was made. In Him was life, and the life was the light of men. And the light
shines in the darkness, and the darkness did not comprehend it.

—John 1:1–5

What Kind of a Friend Are You?

What kind of a friend are you, I say?
When to friends troubles come,
Do you run away?
Do you show them love?
Do you stay true?
Pointing them to Jesus?
Praying them through?
So then, what kind of a friend are you, I ask?
When to friends troubles come,
Do you stay and outlast?

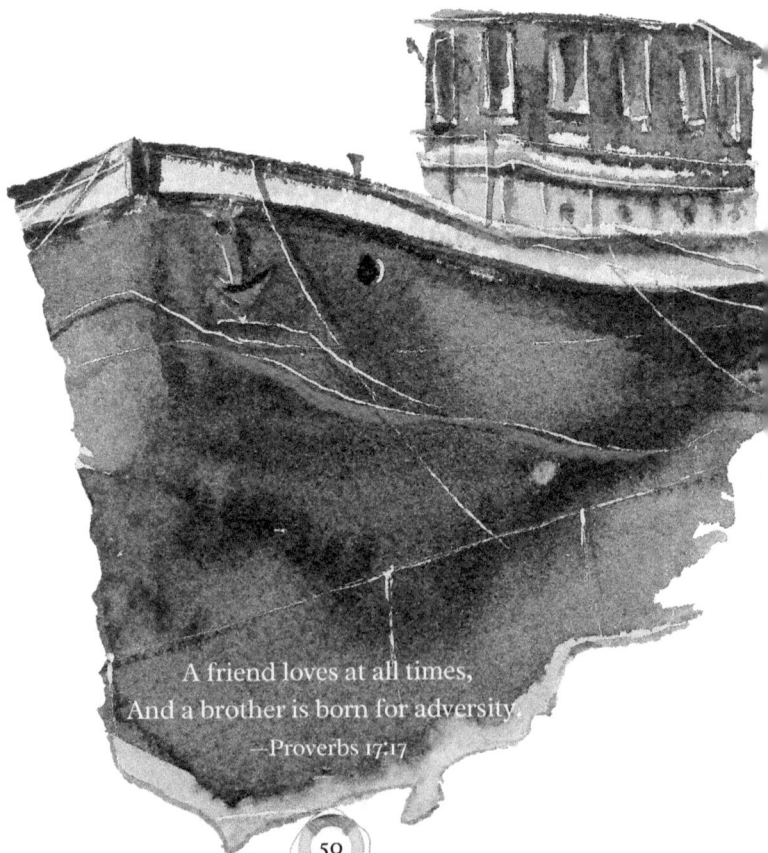

A friend loves at all times,
And a brother is born for adversity.
—Proverbs 17:17

An Orphan's Cry

Can you hear me, sir?
Can you hear me, miss?
Can you bless me financially,
as I roam earth's wilderness?

No money in the bank.
No pillow for my head.
No sheets for a covering.
No mattress for a bed.

No shoes for my feet,
Broken toenails covered in dirt.
My stomach growls for food.
My cold body, in a threadbare shirt.

No one to comfort my aching heart.
No one to hug or hold.
No one to wipe my hot, burning tears.
When sick, no one my fever to behold.

No mama or dada to tell a bedtime story,
or tell about Jesus and all His glory.
Oh, Jesus! Do you hear my aching cry?
To earth You came for such as I.

On the cross, You were orphaned,
bruised and shamed,
You died painfully for us.
So in Heaven, we can be forever named.

So, will you be His arms extended,
reaching out in love?
Will you be His heart outpouring,
tender mercies from above?

Won't you help me, sir?
Won't you help me, miss?
For Jesus' sake, won't you blow me
at least, a financial kiss?

If a brother or sister is naked and destitute of daily food,
and one of you says to them, "Depart in peace, be warmed
and filled," but you do not give them the things which
are needed for the body, what does it profit? Thus also
faith by itself, if it does not have works, is dead.
—James 2:15-17

The Tomb or The Womb?

The tomb or the womb—
what shall it be?
Both are necessary,
if you are to abide in Me.

In your tomb, you bury
your selfish ambitions and desires.
In My womb, you will bear much fruit,
through Holy Ghost fire.

So, tomb or womb—
both it shall be,
birthing My love, joy, and peace,
for now and all eternity.

I am the true vine, and My Father is the vinedresser.
Every branch in Me that does not bear fruit He takes away;
and every branch that bears fruit He prunes, that it may
bear more fruit. You are already clean because of the word
which I have spoken to you. Abide in Me, and I in you.
As the branch cannot bear fruit of itself, unless it abides
in the vine, neither can you, unless you abide in Me. I am
the vine, you are the branches. He who abides in Me, and I
in him, bears much fruit; for without Me you can do nothing.
—John 15:1–5

Valley of Tears

In my valley of tears
where my fears ran free,
stood my gentle Saviour
beckoning me.

Stooped down with cares
my head bent low,
helpless and blinded
my face to the floor.

Then, looking up, I saw
His tender, loving face,
asking me to trust Him
for His much-needed grace.

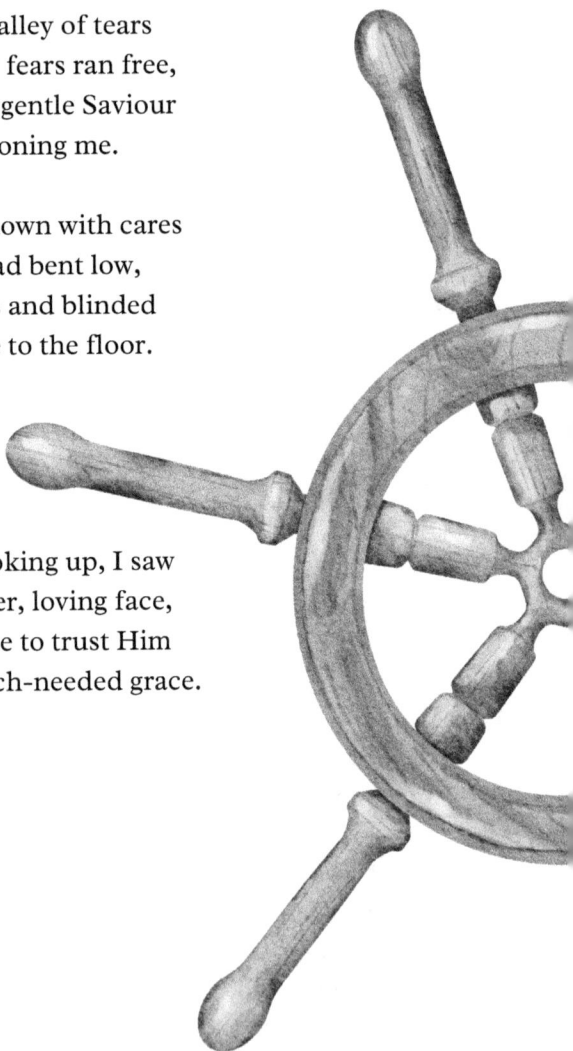

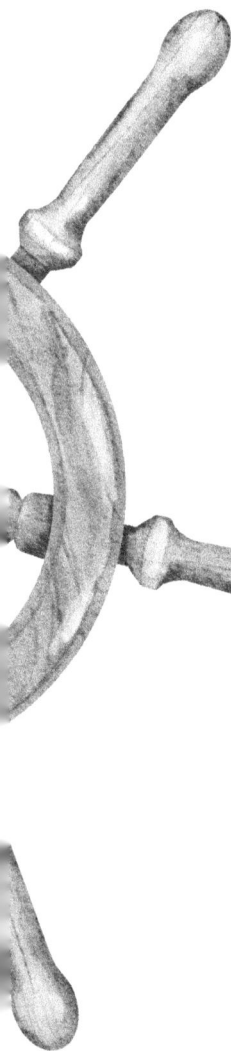

His eye was always on me
even tho' I was unaware,
in my valley of tears
when to the ground, I did stare.

"Your help comes from above.
It is My strength you need.
You will enter My courts
guaranteed to succeed.

I will dry your tears
causing to spring,
blessings abundant
withholding no good thing.

'Cause your soul longs and faints
for Me, all day,
I will not deny you My presence,
But surely lead the way."

Read Psalm 84

Poems of Thanksgiving, Praise, and Worship

Jesus Is His Name

My heart rejoices.
My soul sings.
I delight to praise
my glorious King.

My heart is thankful.
My spirit aflame.
It loves One and One alone,
Jesus Is His name.

He is the Mighty One.
He sits on high.
I need only approach Him
with a gentle sigh.

He opens the windows,
pours down the rain.
I am refreshed and renewed
as I call on His name.

His grace abounds
His love overflows.
My heart can't contain,
and is warmed by the glow.

Enter into His gates with thanksgiving,
And into His courts with praise.
Be thankful to Him, and bless His name.
—Psalm 100:4

A Prayer for Today

Father, I come in humility today,
bless me as I bow my knee and pray.
Bless whatever I think, say, and do.
Bless my family and friends who also need You.
Bless my foes, who against me may say or do,
knowing my comfort and strength is only in You.
No weapon formed against me shall prosper today.
Your angels are also watching each step of my way.

No weapon formed against you shall prosper,
and every tongue which rises against you
in judgment You shall condemn.
—Isaiah 54:17a

Jesus, Lord of a Despairing Heart

I cried out to You in the depths of my despair,
heart aching and wondering if You were there.
I prayed and sought Your face, to find
You are faithful and true and forever kind.

Soothing, comforting, whispering, promising,
Your arms enfolding, Your love entwining.
Grace outpouring, oil overflowing,
upon my despairing heart, bringing healing.

King of Kings and Lord of Lords,
my heavy heart smiles as it looks to You, Dear God.
In Your authority, teach me to walk,
no more afraid or despairing of the enemy's talk.

God is our refuge and strength, A very present help in trouble.
Therefore we will not fear, Even though the earth be removed,
And though the mountains be carried into the midst of the sea;
Though its waters roar and be troubled,
Though the mountains shake with its swelling. Selah
—Psalm 46:1–3

Who Am I, Lord?

Who am I, Lord? that You are mindful of me,
Who am I, Lord? that You changed the course of my destiny.
Who am I, Lord? that You watch and wait for me,
Who am I, Lord? that Your loving arms enfold me.
Who am I, Lord? that Your mercy, love, and grace abounds.
Who am I, Lord? that Your angels surround.
Who am I, Lord? to be fearfully and wonderfully made,
Who am I, Lord? that from sun and moon You shade.
Who am I, Lord? that You convict, cleanse, correct, comfort, and guide.
Who am I, Lord? that to You I can come boldly and confide.
Who am I, Lord? that You befriend me when lost and lonely,
Who am I, Lord? that Your presence is delicious honey.
Who am I, Lord? that You refresh my soul.
Who am I, Lord? that You empower me to reach my goal.

I am but a grain of sand, with the multitudes on the beach;
I am but a speck of dust that You bent down to reach.

It is Your unconditional love for me that burns within my breast.
It is Your Word that transforms me and gives me rest.
It is Your Son, Jesus, who calls me friend.
A great, big, heartfelt "Thank You" to this glorious end.

When I consider Your heavens, the work of Your fingers,
The moon and the stars, which You have ordained,
What is man that You are mindful of him,
And the son of man that You visit him?
For You have made him a little lower than the angels,
And You have crowned him with glory and honor.
You have made him to have dominion over the works of Your hands;
You have put all things under his feet,
All sheep and oxen—Even the beasts of the field,
The birds of the air, And the fish of the sea
That pass through the paths of the seas.
O Lord, our Lord, How excellent is Your name in all the earth!
—Psalm 8:3–9

Father God, Bless Our Home

Father God, bless our home today.
Keep us joyful and healthy, we pray.
Keep our home safe from the wiles of the enemy.
Dispatch Your angels to guard our territory.
Let Your light shine in our home and heart,
blessing those who visit and of us are a part.
Let our conversations be full of grace,
seasoned with salt and gentle of face.
Let our spirits be kind and tender,
hugging heavy hearts, seeking Your answer.
Lord, let Your glory be our crown,
as we don Your love as our earthly gown.
Let the Holy Trinity in our home abide,
wiping every tear and causing every storm to subside.
Let Your presence be real and touch every heart,
flood them with peace and joy even after they depart.

Be anxious for nothing, but in everything by prayer
and supplication, with thanksgiving, let your requests
be made known to God; and the peace of God,
which surpasses all understanding, will guard
your hearts and minds through Christ Jesus.
—Philippians 4:6-7

How Awesome Are You, My God!

How awesome is Your wisdom,
I can scarcely understand.
You did not require man's counsel
when the Heavens and earth, You did span!

How marvelous is Your knowledge,
You filled the earth and sea.
We try to imitate Your creation
in carvings, totally unworthy!

How unsearchable is Your understanding,
Nations are but dust at Your feet.
Kings and judges are brought to naught,
like chaff, blown away in defeat!

How true is Your justice!
How merciful and free!
How much You long to reveal Yourself,
to a worthless grasshopper as me!

When I lift up my eyes to Heaven
and the splendour of Your works, I see.
I have to bow down and acknowledge,
indeed, none can compare to Thee!

Read Isaiah 40:12–28

Poems Based on Biblical Truths

My Heart

I had a heart of stone,
which Jesus took and exchanged it for His own.

He broke the pride to reveal the sin,
that I may be presentable for Him to enter in.

Birthing in it love, mercy, and grace,
tender compassion and a radiant face.

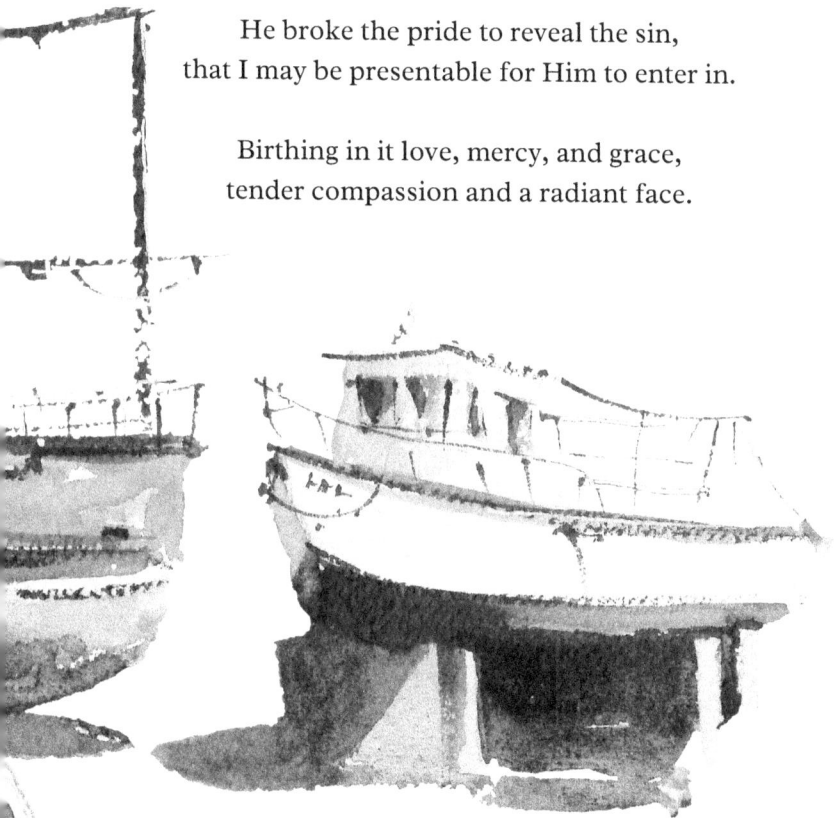

Then I will give them one heart, and I will put a new
spirit within them, and take the stony heart out of
their flesh, and give them a heart of flesh, that they may
walk in My statutes and keep My judgments and do them;
and they shall be My people, and I will be their God.
—Ezekiel 11:19–20

Heaven's Bank

The bank of Heaven is full of tender, loving grace.
The only teller is Jesus, the only cheque is faith.
If my faith is strong, I can be more than sure
the bank will never run dry, and I need not fear.
I can come boldly for help, with arms outstretched too,
looking up to Jesus so faithful and true.

But without faith it is impossible to please Him, for
he who comes to God must believe that He is, and that
He is a rewarder of those who diligently seek Him.
—Hebrews 11:6

Dew Drops from Heaven

Dew drops fall from Heaven
on my parched and thirsty soul,
bringing healing, joy, and refreshing
and helping me reach my goal.

The manna You fed the Israelites
is in Your Word for me.
Instead of feasting on food,
help me feast on promises from Thee.

Apart from pride, it was sight
that tempted Eve to sin.
She looked and saw that the fruit was good,
with Adam brought eternal ruin.

Take my fleshly appetite, Lord
and transform it to a spiritual one,
that will not allow or cause me to rest
till I have heard from You, God's Son.

So He humbled you, allowed you to hunger, and fed you with manna which
you did not know nor did your fathers know, that He might make you know
that man shall not live by bread alone; but man lives by every word that
proceeds from the mouth of the Lord.
—Deuteronomy 8:3

How Blessed I Am in Jesus!

How blessed I am to be Your child of grace.
Jesus' blood and love took away my disgrace.
My scarlet sins were made as white as snow,
dumped into Your sea of forgetfulness,
to be remembered no more.

How blessed I am to be Your child of peace.
By Your word, my every storm must cease.
You neither slumber nor sleep.
I can come boldly to Your throne;
You are waiting for my knock.
You are always home.

How blessed I am to be Your child of love
poured down from Heaven,
from Your throne above.
Where You watch and wait, looking in love
to see that all is well with Your earthly dove.

How blessed I am to be Your child of joy,
joy abundant, eternal, that money cannot buy.
I can sing and skip and dance with glee,
knowing my Blessed Saviour watches over me.

Grace, peace, love, and joy well up in me,
the fruit of Your Spirit, to glorify Thee.

Peace I leave with you, My peace I give to you;
not as the world gives do I give to you. Let not
your heart be troubled, neither let it be afraid.
—John 14:27

Sin

Beware of sin knocking on your door.
It looks tempting, packaged so neat,
looking for a crack to get entry in,
its fruit deceptively sweet.

It attracts, like bees to a honeycomb,
and moths to a flame, to die.
It is addictive, draws insecure hearts,
comfort in wrong places, to buy.

Supposed medicine, for the sick heart and soul.
Often it comes packaged as a sugar-coated pill.
Beware, you will unknowingly swallow—
it will spring on you for the kill.

Sin, a cancerous worm,
eats away and destroys the structure.
Broken lives, shattered dreams,
broken relationships, and families in fracture.

Bad company corrupts good character, the Word says.
Meditate on God's Word; watch your friends.
Use the sword of the Spirit, fight in faith.
Jesus will guide you faithfully to the end.

Do not be deceived:
"Evil company corrupts good habits."
—1 Corinthians 15:33

Your Eternal Fragrance

Your fragrance on earth we see all around,
in the fauna and flora that You cause to abound.
In the autumn, winter, spring, and summer,
in the mountains, valleys, oceans, and sounds of thunder.

But surpassing all these fragrances
is the most precious One.
It is the blood of Your Son,
shed on Calvary for everyone.

The fragrance of Calvary ascended to Your throne,
the sweet savour offering that paid for our ticket home.
Your fragrance of total love, mercy, and grace
broke through sin, death, sickness, and the grave.

The fragrance of salvation, healing, peace, and joy,
defeating the enemy and blessings to enjoy.
The fragrance of Your glorious Word, made real by Your Spirit
to convict and renew and sanctify our minds to Your limit.

Till our fragrance ascends to Your throne on high
the aroma of Christ that brings from You a Heavenly sigh.
"That is My child," You muse, smile, and say,
"Who allows My Son's fragrance to wash,
refresh, and renew each day."

Conform us, Father, to the image of Your Son,
exuding the fragrance of Jesus, till the battle in our lives is won.
That we may be blessed and bless others on our way
to our eternal home, forever with You, to stay.

Now thanks be to God who always leads us in triumph in Christ,
and through us diffuses the fragrance of His knowledge in
every place. For we are to God the fragrance of Christ among
those who are being saved and among those who are perishing.
—2 Corinthians 2:14-15

Your Word

Your Word is pure water;
it washes away my dirt.
It refreshes and cleanses;
it heals my hurt.

Your Word is a mirror
reflecting my spiritual face.
I do not like what I see.
I have to change to run Your race.

Your Word breathes life
into my troubled mind.
It changes my attitudes;
it enables me to be kind.

Your Word brings rebuke and correction;
it works for my good.
It teaches me sound doctrine;
it is Your divine manna, my Godly food.

Your Word is an anchor
that stabilizes me in the storm.
It helps me navigate my way
when winds and waves bring harm.

Your Word is living water
like the Samaritan woman found at the well.
It quenches my spiritual thirst
and has saved me from eternal hell.

Your Word makes all things new;
it saves, restores, refreshes, and renews.
It heals, comforts, guides;
it is everlasting life and is Heavenly dew.

Your Word is a double-edged sword
that enables me in the fight,
to lunge out at the enemy
and change my sorry plight.

Your Word always is, was, and will be.
Your Word is Jesus, who glorifies Thee.

All Scripture is given by inspiration of God, and is
profitable for doctrine, for reproof, for correction,
for instruction in righteousness, that the man of God
may be complete, thoroughly equipped for every good work.
—2 Timothy 3:16–17

The Jailer

As Paul and Silas prayed and sang,
You, Jesus, sent from Heaven an earthly bang
that shook the prison to its core,
loosed shackles and opened doors.

The jailer failed in his duty to keep
the prisoners safe, but instead went to sleep.
His eyes were opened as he saw with fright
what You will do for your children, with might.

He thought Paul and Silas had fled
and wanted to kill himself instead.
But he was surprised to see
that they completely trusted Thee.

Though Paul and Silas were in stocks,
the jailer could freely take a walk.
But Paul and Silas were freely praising Thee
while the jailer was bound in eternity.

He was sound asleep and dead in sin.
Your light brought truth and life to him.
Not just him but his household too;
they all decided to believe in You.

While we suffer hardship and pray,
others with us are blessed on the way.
Sometimes, You allow bad things for a greater good,
though at that time, it is hardly understood.

I can trust You to lead me,
out of injustice to justice
out of bondage to freedom
out of a prison cell to Godly fellowship
out of lack to plenty,
so I can dance with You in glorious liberty.

Dear Jesus, I have fasted, prayed, and believe
You have set my loved ones free
from the clutches of the enemy,
into Your arms, for all eternity.

But at midnight Paul and Silas were praying and singing hymns to
God, and the prisoners were listening to them. Suddenly there was a great
earthquake, so that the foundations of the prison were shaken; and
immediately all the doors were opened and everyone's chains were loosed.
And the keeper of the prison, awaking from sleep and seeing
the prison doors open, supposing the prisoners had fled, drew his sword
and was about to kill himself. But Paul called with a loud
voice, saying, "Do yourself no harm, for we are all here." Then he called for
a light, ran in, and fell down trembling before Paul and Silas. And he
brought them out and said, "Sirs, what must I do to
be saved?" So they said, "Believe on the Lord Jesus Christ, and
you will be saved, you and your household." Then they spoke the
word of the Lord to him and to all who were in his house. And he
took them the same hour of the night and washed their stripes.
And immediately he and all his family were baptized.

—Acts 16:25-33

Five Senses and Conscience

Five senses God gave to natural man
to experience the beauty of His creation.
But more importantly, He gave to spiritual man,
a conscience to judge, before God, if an alien.

Once "born again," the Holy Spirit begins to show,
Jesus and His Word are all he must follow.
If conscience is seared, he will sin.
Rebellion and pride always bring ruin.

All five senses are needed
if natural man is to live a full, earthly life.
Guilt, an essential part of conscience, is needed
if spiritual man is to live an eternal life.

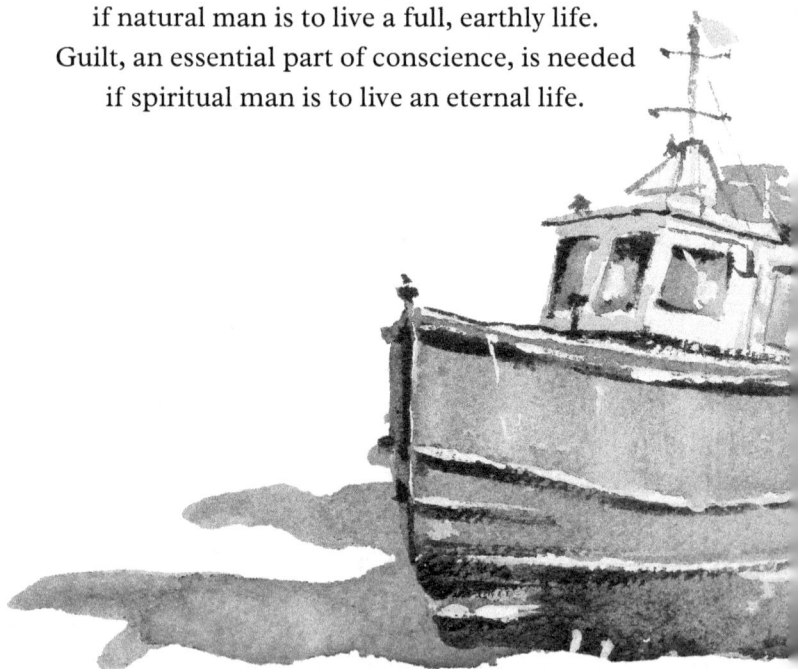

Beloved, if our heart does not condemn us,
we have confidence toward God.
—1 John 3:21

The Resurrection Story

When Adam and Eve in the garden fell,
Father God, You had a plan to conquer hell.
You had to send Your spotless Son
to Calvary, to shed His blood for everyone.

In Gethsemane, He despaired with sorrow,
desiring to give us a better tomorrow.
He sweat blood for the burden of sin,
fulfilling Your will that we may enter in.

He endured the scourging, beating, and mocking,
the spitting, scorning, abuse, and jockeying.
A crown of thorns pierced His head,
deep stripes furrowed His back till He bled.
Nails pierced His hands and feet.
A covering for His body was not even a sheet.

He died in loneliness and rejection,
paying the price for our redemption.
There was no one; He was all alone
as You painfully watched from Heaven's throne.
His disciples, in fear, had fled,
Not understanding what lay ahead.

He cried for water as He thirsted.
They gave Him sour wine and jested,
asking Him to prove He was Your Son
by coming down from the cross, the Holy One.

But little did they know Your plan,
the cross of Calvary—Heaven and earth to span,
our way to You through Your Son,
defeating death and the grave, victory to be won.

The earth for three hours was darkened
as the battle raging in Heaven thickened.
Rocks were split, the temple veil was rent
from top to bottom, all earthly power spent.

He died of exhaustion and gave up His spirit
into Your hands, for He knew Your limit.
He knew He was to rise in glory,
at the appointed time to continue the story.

He was buried in a new tomb, tightly sealed,
for the Jews feared they might be deceived.
Lest the disciples, in their zeal
say He was resurrected, and His body steal.

After the Sabbath, early the next morn,
Mary and the other Mary went to find His body gone.
You sent an angel from Heaven to tell the women
that the Saviour, in majesty and power, had risen.

What joy unspeakable and full of glory
as they rushed to tell the disciples the further story,
of Jesus who was resurrected, as He said,
defeating the enemy, no more blood to shed.

Once and for all, Jesus' blood paid the price
for whosoever believes in Him to rise
and share His glory in Your Heavenly home,
where He sits at Your right hand by the throne.

Jesus, resplendent in power and awesome in Majesty,
King of Kings and Lord of Lords, I worship Thee.

Read Matthew Chapters 26-28

Live for You, Today

Yesterday is gone; there is no need to fear.
May I learn from it and be encouraged to persevere.
Feeling defeated is a waste of time.
You can transform my failures and redeem my time.

Tomorrow has enough troubles of its own.
You know the future—why should I moan?
I may never wake up again, this side of the grave.
Let me walk with You today on a road that You pave.

Today is a day, Father, that You have set.
I come to you, Father, for my needs to be met.
My burden may be heavy, but I can still smile,
knowing that You will go with me each mile.

Let Your presence be with me as I step out the door.
Smile through me today as I face my chores.

Therefore do not worry about tomorrow,
for tomorrow will worry about its own things.
Sufficient for the day is its own trouble.
—Matthew 6:34

The Ocean

One day, I strolled along the beach and saw
the beauty of the ocean, as I gazed in awe.
It was vast and frightening, deep and yet compelling,
wooing me to bathe in its waters, bringing refreshing.

Its mighty waves lashed the shore,
throwing up seashells, pebbles, and so much more.
Like a lion, it roared when the tide was high.
When the tide was low, like a lamb, it was shy.

Its waters reflected the turquoise blue of the sky.
On its beach, passersby could rest, sunbathe, and lie.
The moon and tides governed its course through the day,
all put in place by God, His hand forever to stay.

Awesome in power and majestic in beauty,
purposed by my Creator to fulfill its destiny.
At times, in the ocean, the wrath of God we see
that will be poured out on the ungodly in full fury.

For the wrath of God is revealed from heaven against all
ungodliness and unrighteousness of men, who suppress the
truth in unrighteousness, because what may be known
of God is manifest in them, for God has shown it to them.
—Romans 1:18–19

At Heart, Father God Is a Gardener

As I gaze all around me in nature,
I see the indelible stamp of my Maker.
I am amazed at this beauteous wonder
created for my enjoyment, this majestic splendour.

The seeds lying dormant through the winter,
nurtured by the soil, rain, and sun
burst forth into flowers of spring,
bringing joy to each and every one.

Flowers are gifts to us from our Creator.
They smile and reveal the Father's heart.
He truly, at heart, is a Gardener—
in Eden, He created Adam to start.

All plant life starts with the sowing of a seed,
ensuring continuity of life, indeed!
The same spiritual principle applies to God's Word.
It bears abundant fruit as it is obeyed when heard.

I am the true vine, and My Father is the vinedresser. Every branch in Me
that does not bear fruit He takes away; and every branch that bears fruit He
prunes, that it may bear more fruit.

—John 15:1–2

Sift Me Clean, Lord

Sift me clean, Lord, as You perceive;
pass me as flour through Your holy sieve.
Purge me of grit and stones;
bake me as a loaf for friendly homes.

You are the bread You feed Your flock,
we Your little loaves, whom You prepare for stock
To be distributed as the need arises,
holy communion when the enemy's heat rises.

As the lad with the loaves and fish,
on earth, You gave thanks, broke and multiplied the dish.
Please, take what I have, sift out the leaven,
divinely multiplying, make food for Heaven.

We are Your little loaves, part of Your Body of Bread,
giving life to hungry souls, looking to You to be fed.

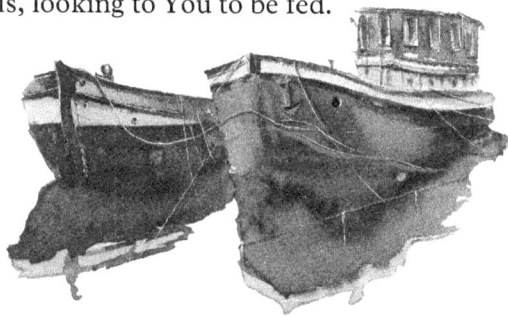

Most assuredly, I say to you, unless a grain of wheat falls
into the ground and dies, it remains alone; but if it dies, it produces much
grain. He who loves his life will lose it, and he
who hates his life in this world will keep it for eternal life.
—John 12:24–25

Unconditional Love in Marriage

Unconditional love in marriage is a must.
That is the only way to earn each other's trust.
The ideal picture for marriage is given by our Saviour,
Who died for the Church, her sole Redeemer.

It was in blood; Jesus paid the price.
Do you think husbands should do otherwise?
To give only when one feels like is not a choice.
It is obedience to God's will that must be voiced.

The home is God's garden, the husband the gardener;
his wife is the flower, gentle and tender.
For the flower to bloom and burst into a smile,
the garden must be right, the soil rich and fertile.

Communication has been cited as the cause of most failures.
It is lack of unconditional love, I believe,
that causes them to flounder.
True commitment is scarce, irresponsibility rife.
Freedom, an excuse, leading to much strife.

He who finds a wife finds favour with the Lord.
He must cherish his garden and turn his attitude to God.
For then only will marriages flourish on earth
and complete the witness of Christ and His Church.

Husbands, love your wives, just as Christ also loved the
church and gave Himself for her, that He might sanctify
and cleanse her with the washing of water by the word.
—Ephesians 5:25–26

Attitude "FOR" God

"Forgiveness, Obedience, Repentance"
is God's three-pronged fork
that should characterize our Christian walk.
Then, from our plate of blessings, we can eat
in joy and peace, watching the enemy retreat.

For the enemy's mission was not just to usurp Adam's seat,
but every child of God he tries to defeat.
However, armed with "FOR," you will see
God working FOR us, causing the enemy to flee.

Behold, to obey is better than sacrifice,
and to heed than the fat of rams.
—1 Samuel 15:22b

If we confess our sins, He is faithful and
just to forgive us our sins and to
cleanse us from all unrighteousness.
—1 John 1:9

Ripple Effect

From the edge of a pond one day, a pebble I threw,
watching concentric circles forming anew,
pushing water outward into the next body, to merge
till the edge of the pond finally broke its surge.

I pondered and thought, herein, a spiritual principle I see.
It's like the law of blessings and
curses that God has laid out for me.
If the pebble I throw into the pond of my life is "sin,"
curses follow, as I have given the enemy a right to come in.
Like the ripple effect,
my sin consequences go down the generation line.
It takes an obedient heart to shake off
the ungodly consequences in time.

If the pebble of "obedience" into the pond of my life I throw,
the enemy has no foothold, and blessings will follow.
God, in His mercy, has limited the ripple effects of "sin."
But for "obedience," to a thousand generations,
blessings flow in.

So, why not choose the pebble of "obedience" instead of "sin?"
By His mercy and grace, I will most definitely shine and win.

For I, the Lord your God, am a jealous God, visiting the iniquity
of the fathers upon the children to the third and fourth
generations of those who hate Me, but showing mercy to
thousands, to those who love Me and keep My commandments.
—Deuteronomy 5:9-10

Prune

My child, hearken to My voice,
and you will see, if you

Pray and praise Me

Root firmly in Me

Unite and knit in Me,

Nations will I give thee to

Extend your hearts in love.

By this lifestyle, I will "PRUNE,"
bringing forth a melodious tune.

Every branch in Me that does not bear fruit
He takes away; and every branch that bears
fruit He prunes, that it may bear more fruit.
I am the vine, you are the branches. He who
abides in Me, and I in him, bears much fruit;
for without Me you can do nothing.

—John 15:2, 5

Be a Giver

Wholeheartedly and cheerfully be a giver.
That's what God's Word says we must do.
Have you stopped to think of your Blessed Saviour
Who, on the cross paid a costly price for you?

Do not nickle and dime with our Sovereign God—
giving should not become bartering.
Naming the harvest is not in God's Word,
best left to Him to decide the blessing.

Blessings will come, that's His Word,
in multiplication, not just simple arithmetic.
He knows what's best for us, in its time,
a harvest of joy we will reap automatic.

Giving should flow out of a generous spirit;
it's the issue of the heart He is after.
So, let's cooperate and do it the Godly way,
for our Father is an abundant giver.

Give, and it will be given to you: good measure,
pressed down, shaken together, and running over will
be put into your bosom. For with the same measure
that you use, it will be measured back to you.
—Luke 6:38

Garment of Praise

We are like various balls of thread,
different colours and textures to fuse.
God is weaving and making out of us,
a "Garment of Praise" for His use.

He patiently weaves the garment by His pattern;
most balls wander off on their own.
Unraveled, they get knotted, broken, or entangled,
till the Master Weaver finally hears their groan.

Lovingly, He irons out the kinks and the knots,
patiently continuing His Heavenly plan.
Each ball has a unique place in the pattern,
collectively, a "Garment of Praise" by God, of man.

For we are His workmanship, created in Christ
Jesus for good works, which God prepared
beforehand that we should walk in them.
—Ephesians 2:10

"FREE-DOM"

Thank you, Lord, for giving us FREE-DOMinion
over the works of the enemy.
Breaking the shackles to set us FREE from DOMination,
overcoming in victory.

You moved us from "down under" to "up over,"
possible because of Your awesome power.
Your blood paid the ticket price for the journey,
from death to life, from defeat to victory.

We are not the tail but the head
walking in Your authority.
We are not victims but victors
marching in Your army.

Stand fast therefore in the liberty by which Christ has made
us free, and do not be entangled again with a yoke of bondage.
—Galatians 5:1

Bowl of Fruit

A bowl of fruit on my dining table lay.
In it were apples, oranges, and pears.
I thought of the fruit of the Spirit
curing my heart of loneliness and despair.

Natural fruit building up the outer man is perishable,
self-conscious, prettying up the outer shell.
Supernatural fruit flowing out of the inner man is imperishable,
God-conscious, blessing others as well.

Natural fruit is grown or bought with the sweat of our brow.
Supernatural fruit cannot be bought; the only way is to allow
the Holy Spirit to tend and oversee the garden of our heart,
pruning and uprooting the unfruitful areas,
causing healthy life to start.

But the fruit of the Spirit is love, joy, peace, longsuffering,
kindness, goodness, faithfulness, gentleness, self-control.
Against such there is no law. And those who are Christ's
have crucified the flesh with its passions and desires.
—Galatians 5:22–24

The Salt of Love

"Be the salt of the earth" is Your command, Lord, to me,
if a flavorful Christian to the world I am to be.
Your Holy Spirit applies the water of Your Word
to draw out my spiritual salt, as it is obeyed when heard.

The heat of the sun draws out salt from seawater,
which was already put in there by You, my Master.
Heat refines all salt and makes it flavorful,
a spice that adds quality to life and makes us thankful.

So is a Christian, without the salt of love,
a poor witness to people of the Lord above.
The salt of love marinates and releases
Godly juices, touching people and lives, in the name of Jesus.

Salt is good, but if the salt loses its flavor,
how will you season it? Have salt in yourselves,
and have peace with one another.
—Mark 9:50

Agape Love

Father, the promises in Your Word
are like fish swimming in an ocean.
Depending on the line I cast out,
with baits of faith, obedience, or forgiveness,
I reel in Your promised portion.

However, the only bait which pleases You,
is the one called "Agape Love."
It is not easy to conquer or master,
but evidences a relationship with You above.

All other baits show a desire for blessings,
maybe cast out in a legalistic spirit.
Father, You know there is no love relationship,
nor a heartfelt desire for fellowship.

Your first commandment is to love You
with all of my heart, soul, and mind.
Your second commandment extends to my neighbour,
to show love and be kind.
To me, the picture above is like a cross,
love flowing up and flowing out as well.
Therein lies the Spirit of victory
that defeated the powers of hell.

Help me focus on You, Lord,
Your fellowship brings peace and abundant joy.
Your nature is to bless Your children
with earthly cares and anxieties, why should I toy?

Teach me to hunger and thirst for You alone,
fulfilling Your righteousness in me.
Teach me to forsake the superficial and carnal,
plunging me into deeper depths in Thee.

You are worthy and awesome,
deserving my all.
But I need Your constant grace,
lest I stumble and fall.

Let the movie screen of my heart,
I pray, tell Jesus' story,
that people getting to view the movie
will desire and thirst for His glory.

You shall love the Lord your God with all your heart,
with all your soul, and with all your strength.
—Deuteronomy 6:5

Where Is Your Heart?

Whom have you trusted your heart with?
Better leave it in the hands of your Maker.
Who really cares about your eternal life?
Only Jesus, your Blessed Redeemer.

For where your treasure is,
there your heart will be also.
—Matthew 6:21

God's Love

Love so immeasurable, love so satisfying,
love so unconquerable, love so energizing.
Love so inexhaustible, love so healing,
love so holy, love so revealing.

Love open in invitation, love personal in call,
love encapsulated in Jesus, who died for all.
Love eternal and forever true,
a breath of fresh air, whispering to you.

Lord, bathe and refresh us in Your love each day,
sent through Your Holy Spirit to ease the way.
Your prescribed medicine for our condition is love,
an antidote to sin, sent from above.

Lord, rain down Your divine manna of love;
let it cascade in floods from Heaven above.
It wipes away tears, it heals our pain,
it is knocking at our door. Will it be in vain?

For God so loved the world that He gave His only
begotten Son, that whoever believes in Him should
not perish but have everlasting life.
—John 3:16

For Those Who Serve

Thank You for Being in "His Ministry of Love"

From the depths of my heart, I want to say
I thank the Lord, Jesus, for each one of you today.
Quietly and gently obeying His call,
marching as one army, extinguishing fires that befall.
As shepherds, I have watched your keen eyes see,
swooping down on the enemy, causing him to flee.

The task is not always easy,
sometimes thankless, the least to say.
Being always of one heart and one mind,
for this, I sincerely pray.

May the glory of the Lord be your crown.
May your joy burst forth, all sorrow to drown.
May your families be blessed in all they do.
May your lives be fruitful with peace and contentment too.

May the Lord guard and guide you each day,
Filling you with His presence, along the way.
May He shower you with His abundant grace from above,
As you serve Him joyfully in "His Ministry of Love."

How then shall they call on Him in whom they have not believed?
And how shall they believe in Him of whom they have not heard?
And how shall they hear without a preacher?
And how shall they preach unless they are sent?
As it is written: "How beautiful are the feet of those who preach the
gospel of peace, Who bring glad tidings of good things!"
—Romans 10:14-15

Acknowledgements

Thank you to Pastor Lennox S. John for the Biblical review.

Thank you, Ruth Hovsepian, for formatting and completing the interior and cover design of this book.

Thank you to Lyneta Smith for editing this manuscript.

Thank you, Andrea Lende, for helping me publish this work.

May the Lord Jesus richly bless all of you!

About the Author

Norma Nazareth was born in Mumbai, India, and immigrated to Canada in the early 1980s. She worked in various financial roles in the private sector and government for three decades.

Norma has always been a truth-seeker and found Jesus when faced with crises in her life and came face-to-face with her mortality. She is a prayer warrior, discipler, and mentor for Christ.

She is currently retired and is called to work with the broken and wounded—the spiritually and emotionally hurting—to bring freedom and wholeness that only Christ offers.

www.ingramcontent.com/pod-product-compliance
Lightning Source LLC
LaVergne TN
LVHW051424080426
835508LV00022B/3227